W9-CCR-925

A New True Book

THE CAYUGA

By Jill D. Duvall

CHILDRENS PRESS®

CHICAGO

J970.4
DUVALL

Cayuga headpiece made
of fur and horns

PHOTO CREDITS

© Jackie Bennett—13 (2 photos), 14, 41

The Bettmann Archive—6

© Reinhard Brucker—2, 12, 23, 25 (left), 26
(left), 29; © Milwaukee Public Museum, 21
(2 photos), 26 (right), 27 (2 photos)

Historical Pictures Service—11

North Wind Picture Archives—8, 16, 19, 20, 25

The Library of Congress, Washington, D.C.—35

© Ron Roels—37

Photograph Courtesy of Smithsonian
Institution National Museum of the American
Indian—31 (left - neg #20823), 40 (neg
#20651), 42 (left - neg #2656)

UPI/Bettmann Newsphotos—33

© 1990 Steve Wall—Cover, 4, 31 (right), 32, 39,
42 (right), 43, 44 (2 photos), 45

© John Kahionhes Fadden—10

Map on page 4—Horizon Graphics

Cover—Cayuga boys playing lacrosse

Library of Congress Cataloging-in-Publication Data

Duvall, Jill D.
  The Cayuga / by Jill D. Duvall.
    p.   cm. — (A New true book)
  Includes index.
  Summary: Describes the history, culture, and
changing fortunes of the Cayuga Indians.
  ISBN 0-516-01123-5
  1. Cayuga Indians—Juvenile literature.
[1. Cayuga Indians. 2. Indians of North
America.] I. Title.
E99.C3D6   1991   91-3038
973'.04975—dc20   CIP
                                       AC

Copyright © 1991 by Childrens Press®, Inc.
All rights reserved. Published simultaneously in Canada.
Printed in the United States of America.
  4 5 6 7 8 9 10 R 00 99 98 97 96

TABLE OF CONTENTS

© 1990 Steve Wall

The Finger Lakes are in western New York State. The original
Cayuga lands (above) were around the shores of Lake Cayuga.

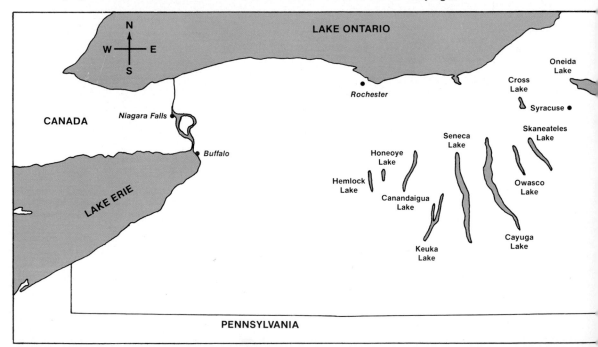

PEOPLE OF
THE MUCKY LAND

Early European explorers called them Cayuga. They called themselves Gueugwehono (goo • way • oh • no) — "People of the Mucky Land." Yearly rains turned much of their territory into marshy wetlands.

The Cayuga lived around Lake Cayuga, which is 66 miles long. It is the longest of the five Finger Lakes of New York State.

Women raised the crops and prepared and cooked the food.

The Cayuga villages were close together. They were connected by trails through the forests. Sometimes the Cayuga had as many as thirteen villages.

IROQUOIS ROOTS

The Cayuga belong to a group called the Iroquois. The Iroquois nations were involved in constant feuds. Some time before the Europeans arrived, a "peacemaker" brought a plan to the Iroquois. Five of the largest and strongest nations agreed to stop fighting with each other.

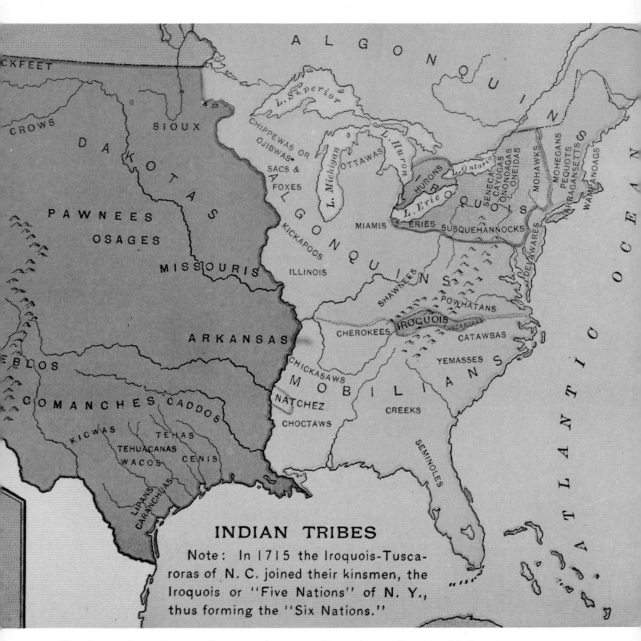

CKFEET

CROWS

DAKOTAS

SIOUX

PAWNEES

OSAGES

MISSOURIS

ARKANSAS

EBLOS

COMANCHES CADDOS

KICWAS

TEHAS

TEHUACANAS

WACOS

CENIS

LIPANS

CARANCHUAS

A L G O N Q U I N

L. Superior

CHIPPEWAS OR
OJIBWAS

L. Huron

SACS &
FOXES

L. Michigan

OTTAWAS

HURONS

L. Ontario

SENECA
CAYUGAS
ONONDAGAS
ONEIDAS

MOHAWKS

MOHEGANS
PEQUOTS
NARRAGANSETTS

WAMPANOAGS

L. Erie

ERIES

SUSQUEHANNOCKS

IROQUOIS

KICKAPOOS

MIAMIS

DELAWARES

ILLINOIS

SHAWNEES

POWHATANS

CHEROKEES

IROQUOIS

TUSCARORAS

CATAWBAS

YEMASSES

CHICKASAWS

M O B I L I A N S

NATCHEZ

CHOCTAWS

CREEKS

SEMINOLES

A T L A N T I C   O C E A N

INDIAN TRIBES

Note: In 1715 the Iroquois-Tusca-
roras of N. C. joined their kinsmen, the
Iroquois or "Five Nations" of N. Y.,
thus forming the "Six Nations."

The Iroquois nations—Seneca, Cayuga, Onondaga, Oneida, Mohawk—
lived in the northeastern woodlands of North America.

The nations were the Mohawk, Oneida, Onondaga, Cayuga, and Seneca.

These nations had territories next to one another in the woodlands of what is now New York State.

The nations formed a league, or confederacy. They called themselves *Haudenosaunee* (ho • dee • no • SAW • nee), the People of the Longhouse. The Europeans called them

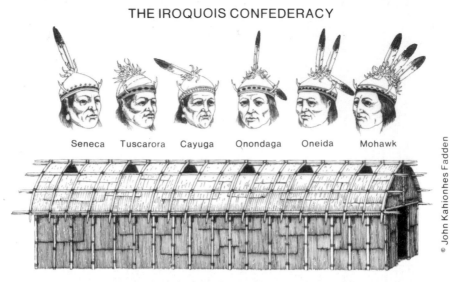

THE IROQUOIS CONFEDERACY

Seneca   Tuscarora   Cayuga   Onondaga   Oneida   Mohawk

© John Kahionhes Fadden

In this drawing by John Kahionhes Fadden, the longhouse represents the Haudenosaunee, or Iroquois Confederacy.

the Five Nations Confederacy or the Iroquois League. Later, the Tuscarora nation joined the Confederacy, which then became known as the Six Nations. People of these nations spoke languages very much alike.

Building an Iroquois longhouse

LONGHOUSE CLANS AND CHIEFS

The early Cayuga lived
in longhouses. Small trees
and saplings were set
in the ground and bent
over at the top to form a   11

roof. Tree bark covered the frame. There was a door at each end of the longhouse. Totems, or emblems, of the clan whose members lived inside were painted over each longhouse door.

Fireplaces were used for cooking and heating in the longhouse.

Cayuga women carry on the clan traditions. The children belong to their mother's clan. The father belongs to a different clan.

Clan members were related through the females. The women who lived in a longhouse were sisters, mothers, or daughters of the same family. The fathers were from a different clan.

Senior Haudenosaunee women were the leaders of their clans. They were called Clan Mothers. Girl babies were always cause for rejoicing because only women could carry on the clans. If there were no females left, the clan died out.

Senior women have always been leaders among the Cayuga.

Clan Mothers arranged
marriages for their sons
and daughters. There were
no marriages among
members of the same
clan.

Ten Cayuga chiefs were
chosen by the Clan
Mothers. When the Iroquois
Confederacy met, these
chiefs represented the
Cayuga. Decisions that
would affect all the
members of the
Confederacy were made at
these meetings.

Europeans came to Iroquois land looking for valuable furs.

NEWCOMERS

Beginning in the seventeenth century, people from Europe came to the Iroquois country. In trading with the Europeans, the Haudenosaunee usually

16

acted together. Dutch,
French, and English fur
trappers all tried very hard
to keep up friendships
with the Iroquois.

Unfortunately, the
Europeans were always
fighting among themselves.
It was not always possible
for the Cayuga to be
friends with all the
newcomers.

Before European colonists arrived, land in North America was never bought or sold. Native Americans used the land but did not think individuals "owned" it. They believed resources were on the land for people to use. The land itself was for future generations to use.

VILLAGE LIFE

Native Americans lived in harmony with nature. For thousands of years, the Cayuga fished, hunted, and trapped around their

The Cayuga loved and respected nature.

19

The forests provided the Cayuga with building materials. Bark was stripped from trees to make canoes and house coverings.

beautiful lake. Their children learned about wild plants and animals in the forest.

Animal skins were made into clothes and blankets. Baskets made from marsh

Woven reed baskets (left) were used
to store food. An Iroquois village
surrounded by a wooden fence (above)
at the Milwaukee Public Museum
in Milwaukee, Wisconsin

reeds were handy for
carrying and storing food.

The Cayuga grew corn,
beans, and squash to eat.
Visits between neighbors
went on all year long.
They shared the foods that
they grew.

21

One favorite time for Cayuga children was the Green Corn Festival. This was held in what we now call the month of August, when the first corn was ready for roasting.

Many families still get together for this festival. There is dancing and singing. Games and contests are held. Food is prepared for days in advance by women and girls.

THE PEACH PIT GAME

Bowl and markers for the Peach Pit Game

A favorite game played at the Green Corn Festival is the Peach Pit Game. Most Iroquois play this game.

The rules of the game are simple. Six peach pits (or other types of counters) are painted with a color on one side. The pits are placed in a wooden bowl. The player raps the bowl sharply against the ground, and the pits bounce. Points are scored on how many pits turn up the same color.

The game may go on for days before there is a winner. People place bets on who the winner will be. Clans often compete with each other.

This game reminds the people that material wealth

Turtle-shell rattles (above).
Games were important to the Cayuga.
Clans often competed with each other.

is not important. Players
bet with a favorite
possession, such as a
ribbon shirt or a turtle
rattle. If this is lost to the
other player, the belief is
that the item will be
waiting for the person in
the "next world."

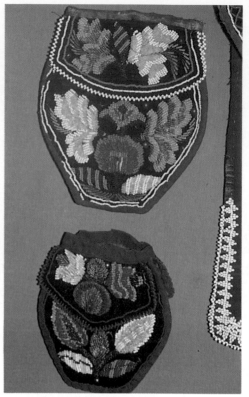

Cayuga soapstone carving of a mask (above). The Iroquois were famous for their beautiful beadwork (right).

The Iroquois have always believed dreams are important. Dream guessing takes place during some Cayuga festivities. A person who has had a dream tells about it in a riddle. People try to guess what the riddle means.

26

Dreams are called wishes of the soul. If someone has had a wish during a dream, the whole nation tries to see that the wish comes true. That way, they believe no harm will come to the dreamer.

The Cayuga used natural materials such as reeds, wood, and animal skins to make baskets (left) and drums (below).

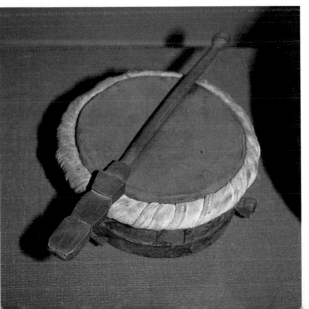

PEACE ENDS

Until the mid-1700s, the Cayuga were able to avoid fights with other members of the Confederacy. From 1700 to 1763, colonial wars followed, one right after another. Dutch, French, English, and Indians were all involved.

In the 1770s the American colonists finally rebelled against England. Life changed rapidly for the Cayuga. Loyalties changed, too.

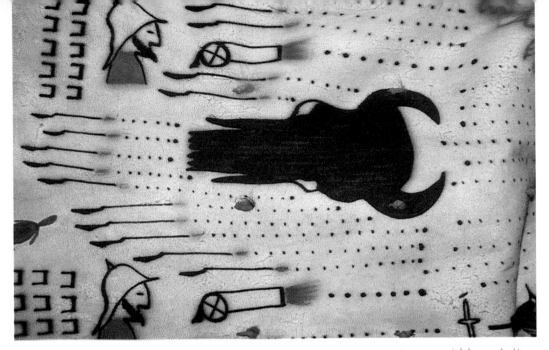

The soldiers and cannons show that this Cayuga hide painting
was made long after the Europeans came to the Iroquois country.

The Confederacy chiefs
could not agree to stay
neutral. Cayuga men
fought on both sides, but
most Cayuga were loyal to
the British.

After the British were
defeated by the American
colonists, the Cayuga

people moved away from their beloved lake. Some joined other Iroquois in Canada. One group moved west to what is now the state of Ohio.

In 1934, their descendants became part of the Seneca-Cayuga Tribe of Oklahoma, where a new constitution has replaced the old laws. A committee is elected every two years to run the affairs of the Seneca-Cayuga Tribe.

Ancient Cayuga lands in

New York State are now filled with non-Indians. This causes great sadness for the proud Cayuga. Yet not all Cayuga have moved far away.

There is still a Cayuga Nation in New York State.

© 1990 Steve Wall

Deskaheb—a Cayuga leader (below). The Iroquois made strings of colored beads called wampum. The beads were often woven into belts in patterns that told a story. Chief Jake Thomas of the Cayuga snipe clan recently accepted the return of sacred wampum belts from the Hcyc Foundation (right).

Cayuga men work on their farm at Grand River on the Six Nations reserve near Brantford, Ontario in Canada.

© 1990 Steve Wall

Right now, they are guests of the Seneca at Cattaraugus Reservation. The Cayuga at Cattaraugus have their own leaders and their clan system. There are many clans among the Cayuga. No one knows just how many clans there are because the Cayuga have been so widely scattered.

"I AM A CAYUGA"

These words were proudly spoken in Europe in 1923. Another "league of nations" had been formed. Members of this league were meeting in Geneva, Switzerland.

The League of Nations meeting in Geneva, Switzerland

Deskaheb, a Cayuga chief of the Younger Bear Clan, was there. He was also called Levi General.

Deskaheb had traveled to Switzerland on a passport issued by the Six Nations reserve in Canada.

The United States president, Woodrow Wilson, dreamed of a League of Nations that would bring about world peace. But to have world peace, small nations must be honored as well as large ones.

President
Woodrow Wilson

Deskaheb wanted to tell
the world leaders that
his own tiny nation was
being treated unfairly.
But the league refused
to hear his speech.

While Deskaheb was in Geneva, Canada proclaimed that the Iroquois government at Six Nations was dissolved. But the Haudenosaunee did not accept the Canadian government's decision. They said that the Six Nations reserve is a separate nation with its own government.

Deskaheb died in exile. When he returned to North America, he was not allowed back into Canada.

Chief Clinton Rickard (in front seat) was a Tuscarora chief who worked hard for the rights of Native Americans. He founded the Indian Defense League, which is still at work.

He went to thc home of a fellow Iroquois, Clinton Rickard. Like his forebears, Clinton Rickard opened his heart to the homeless leader. There, on the

Tuscarora Reservation near Niagara, New York, Deskaheb died on June 25, 1925.

Though Deskaheb never spoke to the league, his words were carried in the hearts of many Iroquois who continued his fight along with Clinton Rickard. Deskaheb was a hero to all Iroquois. Many people throughout the world know of his efforts to help native peoples.

An office in the town of Gowanda, New York, is the symbol of the Cayuga nation, which lost its lands to the early settlers.

© 1990 Steve Wall

A TIME FOR CHANGE

Deskaheb would be proud of his people today. Traditional chiefs, with the help of attorneys, have been able to make significant changes.

In 1974, they convinced
the United States Supreme
Court to make an
important decision. This
decision has changed

A nineteenth-century Cayuga family

Cayuga children at a Christmas party in 1988.

despair into hope for the
Cayuga. The Court said
that Native Americans
have the right to get back
lands taken from them
after the American Revolution. **41**

Lacrosse is an old Iroquois game.
The player at the left wears a traditional
lacrosse outfit. Young players today (right)
wear modern uniforms.

Most of these lands
were taken illegally by
states or by land
companies helped by the
state governments. The
Iroquois were in disarray
then. Most of the chiefs

© 1990 Steve Wall

Painting a pot. Young Cayuga are
keeping the old traditions alive.

had been killed or had
died of disease.

Cayuga territory once
covered millions of acres.
The Cayuga have sued to
get back 64,000 acres of
land. Agreements have been
made, but so far, the lands
have not been returned.

© 1990 Steve Wall

© 1990 Steve Wall

In the game of
Snowsnake (above), a long,
polished pole tipped with
lead is thrown down
an icy trough. The
player whose pole travels
the farthest wins.
Lacrosse sticks (left)
are still handmade
in the traditional way.

Cayuga were among the Iroquois who attended a ceremony in which sacred wampum belts were returned to the Iroquois nations by non-Indians.

Nevertheless, the Cayuga say they will not give up hope of having a homeland again. Their ancestors were buried among the marshes of Lake Cayuga. That is where they want future generations of Cayuga to live.

© 1990 Steve Wall

WORDS YOU SHOULD KNOW

ancestor (AN • sess • ter) — a grandparent or forebear earlier in history

attorney (uh • TER • nee) — a person trained in the law; a lawyer

clan (KLAN) — a group of related families descended from a common ancestor

colonist (KAHL • uh • nist) — a person who goes to another country to live and work

committee (kuh • MIH • tee) — a group of people who work together

compete (kum • PEET) — to take part in a contest

confederacy (kun • FED • er • uh • see) — a union of nations, states, or people joined together for some purpose

constitution (kahn • sti • TOO • shun) — a set of rules or laws for the government of a group of people

descendant (dih • SEN • dint) — a child or a grandchild; a person who comes later in a family line

despair (dis • PAYR) — the lack of hope; discouragement

disarray (dis • ah • RAY) — confusion; disorder

dissolved (dih • ZAHLVD) — broken up; no longer existing

emblem (EM • blim) — a symbol; a thing that stands for an idea

exile (EX • ile) — the condition of being forbidden to return to one's home country

explorer (ex • PLOHR • er) — a person who travels to faroff places to learn about the land and the people there

feud (FYOOD) — fighting; a quarrel, especially one between two groups of people

forebears (FOR • bairz) — ancestors; people who come before in a family line, such as grandparents

generation (jen • eh • RAY • shun) — all the individuals born at about the same time; parents are one generation and children are the next

government (GUV • ern • ment) — a plan for ruling a nation, a state, or a town or city; the people who rule

harmony (HAR • muh • nee) — agreement in feelings or ideas; friendship

illegally (il • LEE • gih • lee) — acting against the law

league (LEEG) — a group of nations or people joined together for some purpose

loyalty (LOY • il • tee) — faithfulness to one's duties, beliefs, friends, etc.

material wealth (muh • TEER • ee • el WELTH) — goods that can be seen, such as clothes and toys, opposed to possessions such as love and friendship

nation (NAY • shun) — a group of people who share a common language, customs, beliefs, and way of life

neutral (NOO • tril) — not favoring one side or the other

passport (PASS • port) — a paper that is issued by a government saying that a person is a citizen of that government's country

proclaimed (pro • CLAYMD) — announced; made public

rebelled (rih • BELD) — rose up against authority; fought to overthrow a government

represent (rep • rih • ZENT) — to act for; to stand for

resources (REE • sor • siz) — supplies of materials such as water or wood, used to take care of people's needs

scattered (SKAT • erd) — spread around; thrown here and there

significant (sig • NIH • fih • kent) — important; having special meaning

territory (TAYR • ih • tor • ee) — an area of land that a group of people regards as their own

totem (TOH • tim) — an animal or a natural object used by a family or other group to represent them; a symbol

traditional (tra • DISH • uh • nil) — following a custom

INDEX

About the Author

Jill Duvall is a political scientist who received an M.A. from Georgetown University in 1976. Since then, her research and writing have included a variety of national and international issues. Among these are world hunger, alternative energy, human rights, cross-cultural and interracial relationships. One of her current endeavors is a study of ancient goddess cultures. Ms. Duvall proudly serves as a member of the Board of Managers of the Glenn Mills Schools, a facility that is revolutionizing methods for rehabilitating male juvenile delinquents.

18 SANDY SPRINGS

J
970.4
DUVALL   Duvall, Jill
             Cayuga.

SANDY SPRINGS

ATLANTA-FULTON PUBLIC LIBRARY
R0089600390

SS   JUL   1999